Books by Dennis M Keating

The Olympics:
An Unauthorized Unsanctioned History

*

Charlie Whitman
Was a Friend of Mine

*

Ena Road

*

The Fulda Gap

*

A Chicago Tale

*

Black Lahu

*

Poetry for Men

1

Ena Road

Murder in
Old Honolulu

Dennis M Keating

This book was created by
the Golden Sphere team
in coordination with the Honolulu Guy,
Dennis M Keating

The Author

Dennis M Keating

THE HONOLULU GUY

DEDICATION

To the victims of
Racism and Prejudice
throughout our world.

ACKNOWLEDMENTS

Thanks to

Professor Steven Taylor
Goldsberry
My Mentor

Paula Marie Fernandez
and Hikari Kimura
For Artwork and Maps

Gail M Baugniet and
Faith Scheideman
Advisors and Proofreaders

Sandy
My Wife, Proponent and Ally

Ena Road

A Narrative Poem
written in
Rhyming Couplets

BY

DENNIS M KEATING

Dennis M Keating, the author of **Ena Road,** has enjoyed a rather peripatetic life. His stories reflect this as each takes place in a different locale – Germany, Thailand, Hawaii, Texas and Chicago.

All five stories are true. Four relate to Keating's personal experiences. The fifth took place almost ninety years ago, but its initial incident occurred just a half block from Keating's current home.

The stories are written for male audiences as they include action, adventure and/or murder in their central themes. They are written in a poetic, rhyming couplet format. Hopefully, this will encourage more men to develop an interest in verse and thereby expand the realm of poetry.

While these tales include gritty elements, many women will also appreciate them. Trustfully, all audiences will find them interesting and compelling.

Ena Road

A lady takes
a midnight stroll.
It ends with the
murder of a man.

Ena Road tells of the *Massie Affair*, a series of events that took place in Honolulu in 1931 and 1932.

The *Massie Affair* concerned a 20-year-old woman with serious emotional and psychological issues, who was assaulted on *Ena Road*. The young lady's jaw was broken. The lady, a Caucasian and, a US Navy Officer's wife, claimed she had also been gang raped by a group of locals. The examining doctors stated a rape did not occur. The local men she accused were of Asian and Polynesian ethnicity. The time line of events showed the locals could not have been at the scene of the crime. The trial resulted in a hung jury, but the story does not end there.

Naturally, racism, prejudice, social status and politics entered the equation. In the end, the Massie Affair had a strong impact on Hawaii and resonated across America to the halls of power in Washington D.C.

In 1931, Hawaii was very segregated. Local Asians and Polynesians did not interact socially with members of the navy or for that matter, any Caucasians.

As the navy, was totally male, virtually all the women at the **Ala Wai Club** were navy wives or family members. Among the sailors, there was sharp competition for the company of the few available females. This resulted in unmarried sailors becoming overly aggressive in their pursuit of single Caucasian women.

During the 1920's and '30's, prostitution was a thriving industry in the Hotel Street and Chinatown areas of downtown Honolulu. While the prostitutes would service both military men and local men, separate waiting rooms were maintained, as the Caucasian sailors did not want to know the woman who they were paying for had previously been with a local man.

Waikiki is approximately three miles from downtown Honolulu. In 1931, Waikiki tourism was a slow growing toddler. Also, Waikiki was small scale. Its clientele was somewhat elitist and pretty much limited to upper classes, movie stars and others with money. Things didn't really change until after World War II, when airplanes rather than ships became the more popular way to cross the Pacific.

Waikiki's first major hotel, the Moana, opened in 1901. A few hundred yards down the beach, around 1915, a group of residential bungalows evolved into the Halekulani Resort. In the mid 1920's, one of its guests, the mystery novel author, Earl Derr Biggers, penned **The House without a Key**, and introduced the world to the fictional Honolulu detective, Charlie Chan. On February 1st, 1927, in between the Moana and the Halekulani, the Royal Hawaiian Hotel opened its doors and became the in place for Hollywood stars and international royalty.

Now, 80 years later, all the participants in **The Massie Affair** are long dead. However, the racism and duplicity entwined in **The Affair** linger on and remain as ghostly shadows that haunt our Land of Aloha.

The author of **Ena Road**, Dennis M Keating, relocated to Honolulu from Chicago nearly 50 years ago. His life in Honolulu, has indirectly been tied to Ena Road. Initially, in 1969 he resided very near Ena Road. Later, he moved on. First, across the island, then, quite literally around the world to the US mainland, Germany, Thailand and then China.

In 2002, after years of travel, Keating returned to Honolulu, again. And once again, his home is just off Ena Road. Because of this proximity and his love of Honolulu, **The Massie Affair** has fascinated his curiosity.

Did little Ena Road
cause Joe to die?

Yes, but only
because of a lady's lie.

Ena Road is just
300 yards long.

Joe was Hawaiian,
young, healthy, and strong.

In truth, he was downed
by a .32 slug,

Fired with hate

by a crazed, hate filled thug.

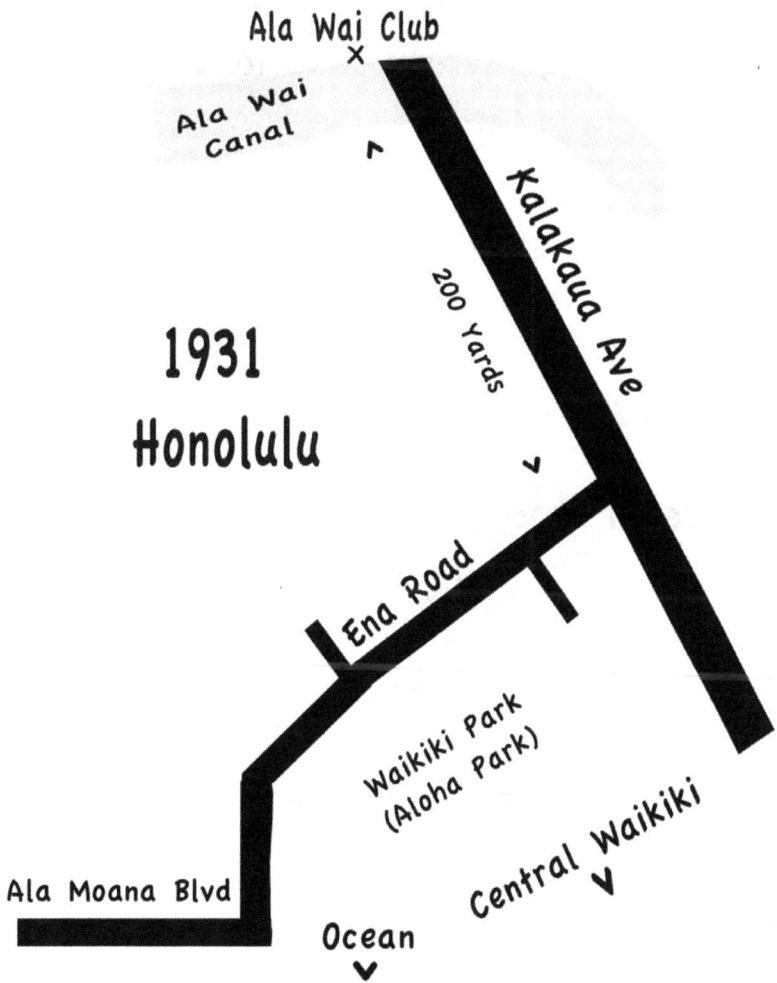

Ala Wai Club
×

Ala Wai Canal

Kalakaua Ave

200 Yards

1931 Honolulu

Ena Road

Waikiki Park
(Aloha Park)

Central Waikiki ∨

Ala Moana Blvd

Ocean ∨

A small .32 slug?
Does that seem strange?

Not really, when discharged
at close range.

Thalia Massie is at the crux
of this tale,

A teen bride, in a marriage
doomed to fail.

She had mental issues
despite being pretty.

To be truly fair,
she deserves our pity.

Ena Road, a minor street on the downtown end of Waikiki, links Kalakaua Avenue and Ala Moana Boulevard. During the 1930's, it housed several small family run shops and restaurants. Also, on the left side, about half way down, there was an amusement park known as Waikiki Park. The park had caravel rides, a penny arcade and a dance hall. It catered to low income Honolulu locals rather than affluent tourists.

In 1928, the dredging of the Ala Wai Canal was completed in order to drain the rice paddies and turn Waikiki into a tourism playground. Waikiki is rectangular. On two sides, it is held in by the Ala Wai Canal. The third side faces Kapiolani Park and the fourth side fronts the ocean.

Thalia's banal husband
left many in doubt.

His ticket to Annapolis?
Won by family clout.

A low-ranking officer
in the Hawaiian fleet,

His success plan:
Lick everyone's feet.

For sure, Thalia got punched
on Ena Road.

Perhaps, it was payback
for a previous goad.

Thalia Massie was Born on St Valentine's Day in 1911. At age 16, on Thanksgiving Day, 1927, she married a Navy Lieutenant. Then, at age 52, on Independence Day eve, 1963, she overdosed and died. In spite of her ties to America's festive days, Thalia was a lonely person who simply never really fit in. She often defied society and, in general, she looked down upon others. Her rebellious acts often seemed to be tied to her personal frustrations, uncertainties and insecurities.

She seemed to detest her privileged life in Washington D.C. and Honolulu. While she disliked being a Navy officer's wife, she seemed to enjoy over indulging in alcohol and getting smashed at parties. Often, she sounded off loudly and rudely insulted others. Unsurprisingly, many Navy wives did not enjoy her companionship.

The culprit?
Probably, a navy man.

She had insulted more than a few
from that clan.

She had berated her spouse
and others shortly before,

Quite likely, one of them
chose to even the score.

Angry and upset, she'd stomped
from the Ala Wai Inn.

Did a sailor follow,
with hopes of sin?

She was found "disheveled"
just off Ena Road.

Her speech tearful,
stuttered, and slowed.

Naturally, everyone thought
the worst case;

Due to her broken jaw
and her bruised face.

Upon examination,
the medics agreed,

She'd suffered a violent,
brutal deed.

The Ala Wai Inn was a restaurant, club and dance hall during the early 1930s. The Inn was located just across the Ala Wai Canal from Waikiki, near the location of the current Hawaii Convention Center, and near the corner of Kapiolani Boulevard and Kalakaua Avenue. On Saturday evenings, the Ala Wai Club was pretty much taken over by the US Navy. If Navy personnel wanted to meet up with each other, this was the place they chose.

But other nastiness
she had escaped.

The doctors concurred.
She had not been raped.

Everyone sympathized.
She was such a pitiful sight.

They didn't take note, how
her story changed during that night.

She blamed five local boys,
but others came to say,

When she was beaten,
those boys were miles away.

Navy Lieutenant Thomas Massie was a graduate of the U. S. Naval Academy in Annapolis, Maryland. In 1927, at age 22, shortly after graduation, he married 16-year-old, Thalia Fortescue. Back home in his small Kentucky town, Tommy was politically connected. He dreamed of making connections in Washington D.C. Thalia's father, a cousin of US President Teddy Roosevelt, had rode with Roosevelt's Rough Riders in Cuba during the Spanish American War. For Tommy, this was a political match made in heaven.

Tommy had been a so-so student at the Naval Academy and was proving to be a mediocre and unimpressive naval officer. Inside, he realized this. He knew his opportunities for advancement were tied to his being friends with everyone, especially those higher up the ladder.

For sure, Joe Kahahawai
was not in Waikiki.

Third-party testimony proved
he just couldn't be.

The only logical conclusion:
the lady chose to lie.

For this prevarication,
Joe was doomed to die.

Facts and timelines
were ignored by the naval elite.

Admiral Stirling, the Navy Poobah,
spoke for the fleet.

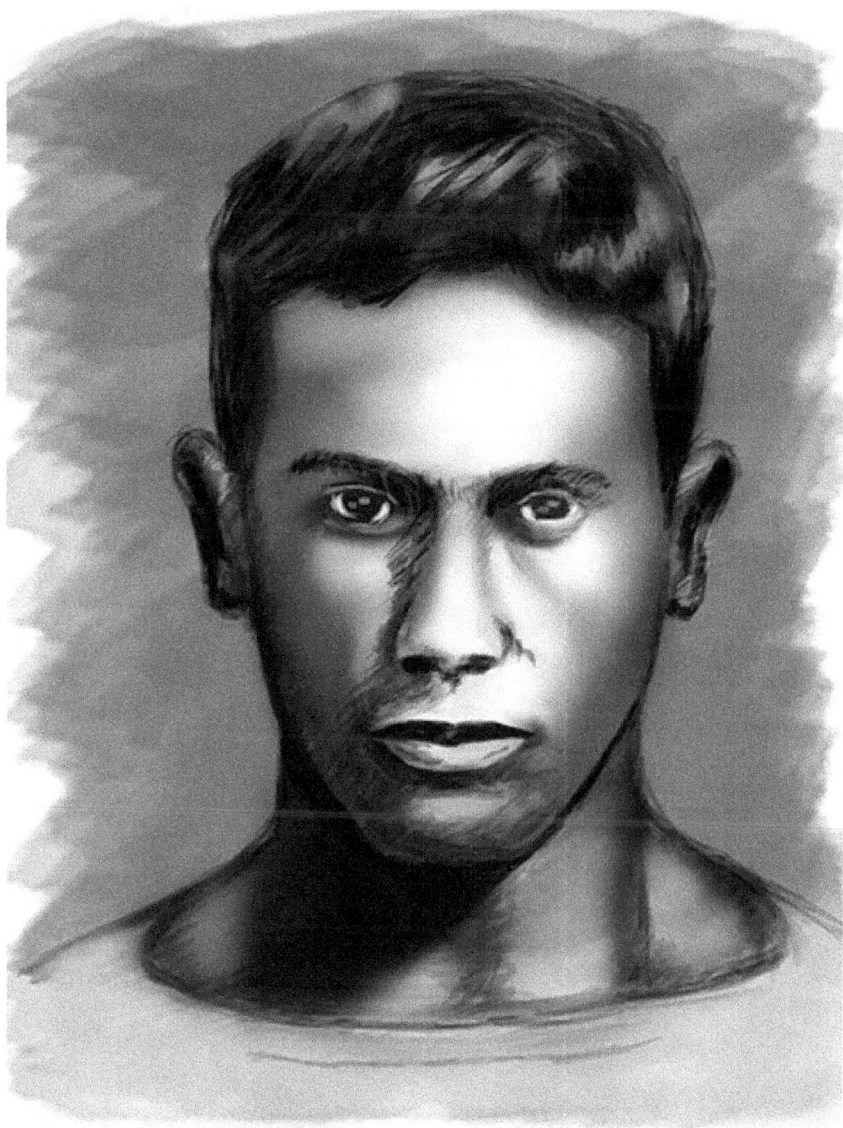

Joe Kahahawai

These brown-skins are savages.
Bring them to their knees.

Better yet, just get some ropes.
Hang 'em from the trees.

Thalia's mother? A self-styled
East Coast, Blue Blood.

Brown-skins were evil.
Navy men? Low-class scud.

Thalia, dazzled by her husband,
as a teenage lass;

Now, five years wiser, realized
he could only kiss ass.

The five young men accused by Thalia Massie:

Joseph Kahahawai - 20 years old

Ben Ahakuelo - 20 years old

Horace Ida - 24 years old

Henry Chang - 22 years old

David Takai - 21 years old

Thalia hated the Navy,
its fleet and its subs.

Her rude comments made her
unwelcome at navy wives clubs.

To Thalia, Oahu was
Just a lonely rock pile.

"How do I get off
this desolate isle?"

No surprise,
Thalia left the party alone.

Did a young sailor follow?
Someone she'd known?

Facts concerning Thalia Massie on the evening of Saturday, September 12, 1931.

Thalia and her husband, Tommy, joined other navy personnel at the Ala Wai Inn after having a few drinks at their home, three miles away, in the Manoa section of Honolulu. This was a regular thing for them, because Saturday evening was virtually Navy Night at the Ala Wai Inn. During the evening, Thalia and Tom, as usual, didn't hang out together. Thalia got into an argument with another navy officer and slapped his face. Later, after 11:00PM she left the Inn alone. She crossed the Kalakaua Avenue bridge behind the club and walked one block to Ena Road. It seems, some person on Ena Road, for some reason, slugged Thalia hard enough to break her jaw. The actual circumstance has never been determined.

Did his sensitive ear
lead to a sensual paw?

Did she yell, "Bug off!"
and he, then, smacked her jaw?

Maybe, Thalia slapped back
and he hit her again.

He then hurried off,
leaving her dazed and chagrin.

When her husband saw her,
he let out a shout.
She was injured, bloody,
and full of doubt.

Who slugged her? Her husband? She'd embarrassed him many times. Another Navy guy who followed her? Quite possible. A local guy on Ena Road? Also, possible. Only she and the assailant knew. That night, she changed her tale several times. Finally, it was, "This is my story. And, I'm sticking with it."

Her tale concerning the five local guys didn't hold water. She claimed she'd been dragged into the weeds and raped, yet her dress was neat and clean. The examining doctors stated she was not raped. Those five guys were involved in a traffic incident, three miles away, at the same time she was slugged. She'd read and heard police reports on the guys, before revising her story. The police reports included a license plate number and other details that she added to her tale.

If the truth showed
a navy man did this,

Rumors would fly. "Ooh là là!
Thalia's having a tryst."

She and her hubby would be dragged
through the dirt.

Better to claim those local savages
wanted under her skirt.

The police had picked up
five locals for another fight.

Blame these guys. Then the cops
would lock it tight.

Had a more thorough police investigation been done, the whole Massie Affair would have never occurred.

Forget that. We all know, sex, violence and the honor of white women sells newspapers. Add tales of jungle savages and the mysteries of the Pacific islands and every major newspaper in America pushed the story to the front pages.

The US mainland press followed the lead of the Honolulu papers and the Navy Commandant. They all came down 100% against the local defendants.

The national press chose to depict local Hawaii residents as uncivilized, jungle barbarians. The press and many national politicians advocated placing Hawaii under the rule of military marital law.

Logic and reason
flew over the wall.

White women's honor
became the Navy's battle call.

The military brass? "Hang, yes hang
these rapists for their deed."

The Honolulu newspapers?
"Guilty" in every lead.

Mainland media?
Jumped on the "Guilty" cause.

Jungle beasts deserve death.
They live without laws.

The US mainland press portrayed Hawaii
as a lawless, uncivilized place.

When the case came to court,
the jury just viewed facts.

The prosecutor's case
was full of leaks and cracks.

Most jurors were local,
so the Haole elite cried foul.

"These brown-skins protect
each other!" they howled.

The Hung Jury verdict
shocked mainland USA.

"Lawlessness rules in
those islands far away.

Reflective the US press reports, the Kentucky House of Representatives on January 18, 1932 adopted Resolution H. R. 11, requesting that US President, Herbert Hoover, take action to bring Hawaii under martial law and make it safe for women. The resolution stated in part:

". In September last, the wife of Lieutenant Thomas Hedges Massie, an officer in the United States Navy and a native and citizen of Winchester, Kentucky, stationed at Honolulu in Hawaii, was kidnapped, assaulted, beat, mangled, her jaw broken and raped six times by five Oriental native Hawaiians, resulting in pregnancy, confining her to a hospital, and making an operation for abortion imperative. Although she identified four of the five rapists, the jury which tried them, failed to convict, leaving this foul and horrible crime unpunished. . ."

White women aren't safe
in that primitive place.

Dark-skins lack the morals
of our superior race."

The press, upper class,
and military spoke as one:

"All five are guilty.

God demands justice be done."

Thalia's mother pushed Tommy

into a devious plot.

"Thalia's honor's been trashed.
We must remove this blot."

Rear Admiral Yates Stirling was the powerful Commandant of the Fourteenth Naval District and top honcho at Pearl Harbor. He believed the five local men were totally guilty and did not let the facts get in the way of his opinions. He publicly proclaimed his position with numerous racist comments. His statements and his strong displeasure with the hung jury, encouraged the sailors under his command to take physical action against the accused men. His opinions set the tone for the positions taken by the local and national press.

"We know Joe Kahahawai
was the lead guy.

Force him to confess;
then all five will fry."

With a phony summons & rented car,

they grabbed Joe.

"Just stick a pistol in his gut.
Act fast. No one will know."

Joe was tied down and beaten
more than a bit.

To survive, Joe figured
"I gotta try to split."

In 1930, Hawaii's population of 370,00. The majority were Asians brought over to work the sugar cane fields. Caucasians were in the minority, but controlled the power structure. Most Caucasians, or Haoles, as they are referred to locally, resided on Oahu, in Honolulu. Most of the US military were also stationed on Oahu. Basically, Haoles controlled the political, economic and social structure of Hawaii.

The Haole establishment was eager to have the whole *Massie Affair* resolved as quickly as possible. Yes, there was a rush to judgment. The Haole Establishment believed of Thalia's inconsistencies and confusion of facts, was due to the traumatic experience she endured and not because she chose to misrepresent or fabricate events.

Joe lunged.
The gun fired hot lead.

Within seconds,
Joe hit the floor, dead.

"Better dump the body
out by Blowhole."

The police, tailing them,
halted that goal.

With a nude corpse in back,
their alibi was lame.

The henchmen gang
had no one to blame.

Thalia's mother, Grace Fortescue was a New York City socialite and a relative of Alexander Graham Bell of telephone fame. Grace had numerous political and social connections in New York as well as Washington D. C. When the Massie Affair started, she had immediately sailed to Hawaii to support her daughter. She then rented a home near her daughter's home.

Grace was the main protagonist in the planning, organizing and kidnapping of Joe Kahahawai. Due to her connections, back on the East coast, she was able to induce famed criminal lawyer, Clarence Darrow to come out of retirement and defend her and the other defendants in the murder trial.

This caused a second trial
in the Massie Case,

"Murder One!"
was the new charge to face.

Get famed lawyer, Clarence Darrow,
"He'll save the day."

No luck. Factual evidence
dwarfed what Darrow could say.

The jury and judge
decided once again.

"The haoles are guilty.
Ten years in the pen."

In 1931, Clarence Darrow, undoubtedly was the most famous lawyer in America. He had already been retired several years and was well into his 70's, when he was approached to take the Massie Case.

Apparently, Darrow took the case and came out of retirement for two reasons. One, due to the stock market crash of 1929 he had lost much of his savings. He was near broke and simply needed the money. Two, he had never been to the islands and Hawaii was on his bucket list.

Normally, Darrow chose to defend the downtrodden. This time, he threw in his lot with the establishment. It is interesting how money is often the guiding light of one's moral compass.

No way!
The white establishment cried "No!"

So, with one-hour house arrest,
Governor Judd let them go.

The killers partied
late that night.

Totally free,
they made jokes of their plight:

White man's purity
had saved them from jail.

Days later, to San Francisco,
they all set sail.

JOSEPH
KAHAHAWAI Jr
BORN DEC 25 1909
KILLED JAN 8 1932

Now, some eighty years have passed;
The players have met their fate.

The Massie Case is legend;
And Hawaii's now the 50th state.

As for poor Joe, his body lies
in Kalihi, under six feet.

Buried in Puea Cemetery,
just off School Street.

No surprise, Thalia's marriage
took a downward course,

It ended two years later
with a Reno divorce.

Aftermath - Thalia

At the Reno divorce court, Thalia told the press, she would never marry again. Later that evening, she went back to her hotel room and attempted a drug overdose. Both her attempted suicide and her plan to stay single were unsuccessful. In 1953, at age 42, Thalia did marry again. This time she chose a 21-year-old college student who had not yet been born when the whole Massie Affair started. No surprise, her second marriage was a short one.

Over the years, she tried to commit suicide numerous times. Finally, at age 52, her last suicide attempt was successful and her sad life ended.

With suicide concerns,
her family kept her close.

Then, in 1963, her sad life ended:
a drug overdose.

Today, Hawaii evolves,
mostly for the good.

Race issues are better,
not as ideal as they should.

True, the Massie Affair,

Happened many years ago,

But to truly know our islands,
It's something you should know.

Aftermath – Joe Kahahawai

Joe's Kahahawai was born Christmas Day, December 25, 1909 and murdered twenty-two years and two weeks later on January 8, 1932.

Joe, a Catholic, had attended St Louis high school through a football scholarship. He was an active athlete in other sports including boxing.

His funeral mass was held at the Lady of Peace Cathedral in downtown Honolulu. After the service, the pallbearers carried Joe's casket by hand, two miles to Puea Cemetery in the Kalihi neighborhood of Honolulu. There, a second service was held. It was stated that more than 1,000 individuals attended the service and that it was the largest funeral service since the death of Hawaii's last queen, Queen Liliuokalani, fourteen years earlier.

Aftermath - Tommy

Tommy fared little better than Thalia. He married again in 1937. While his second wife did not have psychological issues, she got embroiled in an international incident in Tsingtao, China a year after their marriage. After visiting Tommy aboard his ship, she returned to a pier where a Japanese sentry slapped her in the face for failing to comply with his Japanese language orders.

Unfortunately, Tommy's whole life continued to crumble. He began to show signs of psychiatric disorders. His condition got worse and prior to World War II the Navy decided to release him from active duty. Tommy lived until 1987, but his life was a sad and bitter one.

Aftermath – Grace Fortescue

Thalia's mother, Grace, orchestrated the whole plot to kidnap Joe Kahahawai. Unlike, Thalia and Tommy, the whole Massie Affair really never phased her.

Grace shrugged off her manslaughter conviction for killing an innocent man and returned to her socialite role on the East Coast. She was not shy to discuss, in her words, "the murder."

Two years after the Massie Affair, she inherited her full share of the Bell estate and bought a house in the Bahamas. She lived a full active life as a rich widow, well into her nineties. Thanks to her deceased husband's military service, this key plotter in Joseph Kahahawai's murder was honored by our nation and buried at Arlington National Cemetery.

The Ballad of Joe Kahahawai
A poem by Dennis M Keating
Copyright © 2017 Dennis M Keating

**If you wish to accompany this poem with a
guitar, recommend using a tune similar to
The Night They Drove Old Dixie Down
by Robbie Robertson**

Joe Kahahawai was his name,
And he came from the Valley Isle.
While restless and untame,
He won many friends with his warm smile.

The day they shot poor Joe down;
His killers were driven by hate.
The day they shot poor Joe down;
It changed our island's fate.
And we cried, "No, na, na, na, na, no."

Joe was just 22, proud and brave;
When that .32 slug laid him in his grave.
It was all due to the lady's lie
That Joe became an innocent fall guy.

The day they shot poor Joe down;
His killers were driven by hate.
The day they shot poor Joe down;
It changed our island's fate.
And we cried, "No, na, na, na, na, no.

It was January of 1932.
With one slug to his chest; Joe was through.
They'd kidnapped Joe near the courthouse;
They said to avenge a wronged spouse.

The night the lady cried, "Rape!"
All the whites were teeming.
The night the lady cried, "Rape!"
All the news headlines were screaming.
They screamed, "No, na, na, na, na no."

Back in Kalihi, Joe's mother cried.
She'd lost her hope, her dream and pride.
"Oh, dear God! Set me free!"
"My only son's been taken from me."

The day they shot poor Joe down
His killers were driven by hate.
The day they shot poor Joe down
It changed our island's fate.
We cried, "No, na, na, na, na, no."

"Now I don't mind my hotel job.
Sure, I kowtow to some mainland snobs.
While they talk down to me, at night I can rest.
But God, why have you taken my very best."

The Day they buried Joe Kahahawai;
All the Hawaiians marched proudly.
The Day they buried Joe Kahahawai
All the women wailed loudly.
They wailed, "No, na, na, na, na, no."

The court told the killers "You're guilty!"
And gave them ten years in the pen.
But, Governor Judd said, "I'll make you free.
Just wait an hour and, you're on the street again."

The day they let the killers free;
It was Hawaii's death knell.
The day they let the killers free,
Was the day, Hawaii's soul went to hell!
We all cried, "No, na, na, na, na, no."

ABOUT THE AUTHOR

Dennis M Keating has enjoyed a peripatetic lifestyle. His international perspective and eclectic enthusiasm for life come from his forty some years in Germany; Thailand; China and Hawaii.

For the last ten years, Keating and his wife, Sandy, have been living a quiet life in Waikiki. Normally, he can be found pounding his iMac keyboard, hiking the Diamond Head trail, or strolling with his wife at sunset along the sands of Waikiki.

Keating writes on a diverse range of topics. His books draw upon his multifarious interests and personal experiences. Most of his books are nonfiction.

Keating's Facebook page:
https://www.facebook.com/TheHonoluluGuy/
He is happy to Friend you on Facebook.
In 2016, Keating released - *The Olympics: An Unauthorized Unsanctioned History*

In 2017, Keating released
Poetry for Men - Action Adventure Murder is a compilation of Keating's five poetry books.

Charlie Whitman was a Friend of Mine. The story of the Texas Tower Killer.

Ena Road. Murder and racism in Hawaii.

The Fulda Gap. A Cold War confrontation.

A Chicago Tale. A triple murder story.

Black Lahu. Opium, life and death in the Golden Triangle.

His email is **lostpuka@gmail.com**
His websites are:
GoldenSphere.com & **HonoluluGuy.com**

Keating owns all rights to the material in this book. For film rights, or for other reasons, please contact him.

www.ingramcontent.com/pod-product-compliance
Lightning Source LLC
Chambersburg PA
CBHW060636280326
41933CB00012B/2065